This book
belongs to

_____

_____

Picture Kelpies is an imprint of Floris Books
First published in 2013 by Floris Books
Second printing 2014

The publisher acknowledges subsidy from
Creative Scotland towards the publication of this volume
British Library CIP Data available
ISBN 978-178250-003-2
Printed in China through Asia Pacific Offset Ltd

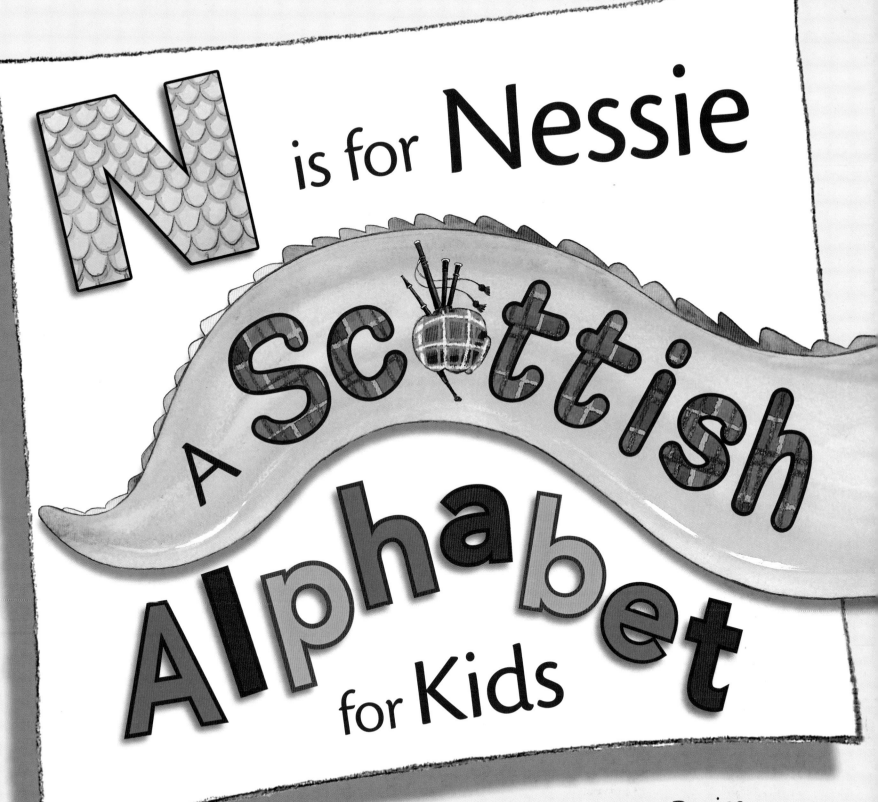

N is for Nessie

A Scottish Alphabet for Kids

Illustrated by Kate Davies

Auld Lang Syne

Bagpipes

Castles

Dogs

Eagle

Forth Bridge

Golf

Highland cow

islands

John O'Groats

JOHN O'GROATS

Kilt

Loch

Midgie

Oats

Puffins

MARY

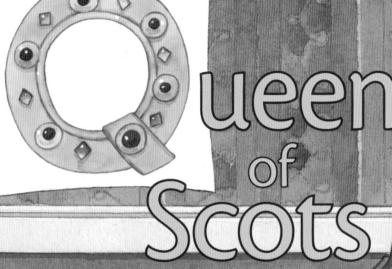ueen
of
Scots

Red squirrel

Stag

Thistle

Umbrella

Very, very wet

Yarn

Find out more about Scotland

Auld Lang Syne is a poem by Scotland's most famous poet, Robert Burns, that is sung at Hogmanay.

Bagpipes are the most famous musical instruments in Scotland.

Castles are found all over Scotland. This book shows Stirling Castle, Culzean Castle in Ayrshire, and Urquhart Castle on the banks of Loch Ness.

The three Scottish **dogs** in this book are a Scottie (Scottish Terrier), a Westie (West Highland White Terrier), and a Scottish Deerhound.

The Golden **eagle** is a large bird of prey that lives in the Scottish Highlands.

The Forth Bridge takes trains between Edinburgh and the north.

Golf was invented in Scotland.

Highland cows have long horns and thick hair to keep them warm in the Scottish winter.

Scotland's islands are some of the wildest and most beautiful in the world.

John O'Groats is the most northern town of mainland Britain.

A **kilt** is like a man's skirt made from tartan cloth.

Loch is the Scottish word for a lake. Some of the most famous lochs in Scotland are Loch Lomond and Loch Ness, home of Nessie.

A **midgie** is a biting insect that lives in Scotland.

Nessie the Loch Ness Monster is a mythical creature that famously lives in Loch Ness, near Inverness.

Oats are used to make famous Scottish foods like porridge, bannocks, oatcakes, black pudding and haggis.

Puffins live all around the coast of Scotland but big colonies can be found on the Isle of May and St Kilda.

Mary **Queen of Scots**, also known as Mary Stuart, was a famous Scottish queen.

Red squirrels live in the north of Scotland, safe from grey squirrels.

A **stag** is a male deer which lives in the Scottish Highlands.

The **thistle** is the flower symbol of Scotland.

Scotland is well known for being **very, very wet** so remember to bring your **umbrella**!

Whisky is a popular drink made in Scotland.

X is the shape in the Saltire flag, the flag of Scotland.

Yarn is used for knitting warm jumpers, socks and lots of other things.

Edinburgh **Zoo** is home to Scotland's first pandas and a happy group of parading penguins.